# CONFRONTING
# LIES &
# HATE

## Responding With Truth And Grace

### ROBERT H. KNIGHT

D. JAMES
KENNEDY
MINISTRIES

Fort Lauderdale, FL

Confronting Lies & Hate
*Responding with Truth and Grace*

By Robert Knight

ISBN: 978-1-929626-80-9

Cover and Interior Design: Roark Creative, www.roarkcreative.com

Printed in the United States of America.

Published by:

D. James Kennedy Ministries
P.O. Box 11786
Fort Lauderdale, FL 33339
1-800-988-7884
DJKM.org
letters@djkm.org

# CONTENTS

*"A soft answer turns away wrath,
but a harsh word stirs up anger."*

– Proverbs 15:1 (ESV)


*"Dear children, let us not love with words
or speech, but with actions and in truth"*
– 1 John 3:18

# INTRODUCTION

*"Anger is a weed; hate is the tree."*
– St. Augustine

As a God-given human emotion, hate is neither good nor bad. Its value depends on how, when, and why it is expressed.

The word "hate" is often harmlessly used to vent merely strong feelings of dislike, such as, "I hate it when it rains on the weekend." It's also used to express deeply negative feelings that rise up from our souls and circumstances, warranted or not. Hate can be soothed by love, or it can be stoked with anger.

In country music, which thrives on telling stories, hate is a recurring theme and vital element. Johnny Cash once said, "Of emotions, of love, of breakup, of love and hate and death and dying, mama, apple pie, and the whole thing—it covers a lot of territory, country music does."

In this passage, C.S. Lewis describes what is hateable; that is, what deserves to be hated:

> Christianity does not want us to reduce by one atom the hatred we feel for cruelty and treachery. We ought to hate them. Not one word of what we have said about them needs to be unsaid. But it does want us to hate them in the same way in which we hate things in ourselves: being sorry that the man should have done such things, and hoping, if it is anyway possible, that somehow, sometime, somewhere he can be cured and made human again.[1]

And there's the difference between the world's response to hate and that of the Christian. The world seeks vengeance, returning hate for hate; the Christian is told to return love for hate and to work toward redemption, even of our enemies.

In the Sermon on the Mount, Jesus made this clear: "*Love your enemies, bless them that curse you, do good to them that hate you, and pray for them which despitefully use you, and persecute you*" (Matthew 5:44).

In recent years, hate has taken on a new meaning. It seems to be everywhere in the news these days, and not by happenstance. The charge of "hate" or "hatred" has become a weapon of the Left in the cultural and political wars. Increasingly, campus protesters and even members of Congress have shut down debate by accusing opponents of being motivated solely by hate. It's a difficult charge to answer, but there are effective ways to do so, as we will see later.

The purpose of this book is to examine what's behind the increasingly vitriolic and false accusation that defenders of traditional values, and Christians in particular, "hate" those with whom we disagree, and to offer ways to counter it.

While some people honestly believe that Christians harbor hatred, others cynically deploy the charge in order to intimidate and silence their opponents. They know that Christians are not hateful, but say it anyway because it works. Who wants to be known as a "hater"?

When pressed to the wall, even devout Christians will often surrender moral ground in an attempt to deflect the "hate" charge. It doesn't work, and invites more attacks, but it is a natural response that we must actively discourage in the face of pressure to conform to the world's standards.

Jesus instructed us to turn the other cheek. That means not to take the bait and rise in like manner to every provocation, but instead, to exhibit patience and restraint. It doesn't mean, however, to become a doormat for abuse of any kind or to give up trying to counter lies with the truth. The dangers of that approach will be addressed in Chapter Three.

The first thing to do when confronted with outright lies, such as the false charge of hate, is to see what God has to say about it. So in Chapter One, "The Biblical View," we will explore the Scriptures' view of hate and love. It might be tempting to say something like, "hate comes from Satan, while love comes from God," but it would not be true. Both emotions come from God, since Satan cannot create anything. The best that Satan can do is to corrupt God's good creation, and that includes fanning the flames of hate for wrongful purposes.

In Chapter Two, "Miscasting Christianity," we will look at ways that opponents mischaracterize Christians and Christianity. From negative media portrayals to films featuring Christians or Christian-like people as villains, a picture is emerging as an American subgroup that is, at the least, annoyingly ignorant and perhaps even threatening.

Chapter Three, "From Ridicule to Genocide," relates how an otherwise educated country—Germany—fell sway to a philosophy of racial superiority that ended in mass murder, and why it is a cautionary tale for Americans.

Chapter Four, "Hate Crimes: What Were You Thinking?" delves into the rise and abuse of so-called hate crime laws and policies. What might seem at first to be a welcome addition to the crime-fighting toolbox actually takes the law selectively into realms that were long considered private—such as conscience.

Chapter Five, "Deploying Hate as a Political Weapon," explains how allegations of hate are being used to silence conservative voices, not just those of Christians. It is part of an overall leftist cultural strategy to overthrow Western civilization, which will be examined in Chapter Six, "The Rise of Cultural Marxism."

Chapter Seven reveals the dangerous campaign by the Southern Poverty Law Center to silence Christian groups (including D. James Kennedy Ministries) by falsely designating them as "hate groups." Finally, Chapter Eight, "Responding with Truth and Grace," offers ways for Christians to counter the Left's most frequently used tactics of lies and character assassination.

The best defenses against lies and hate are facts and love. Unjust accusations may cause havoc for a time, but most are eventually found out. The tone of our responses is profoundly important. Proverbs 15:1, says, "*A soft word turns away wrath, but a harsh word stirs up anger.*" This applies when we tell the truth in love, which is sometimes a long overdue corrective.

Although the adage, "A lie gets halfway around the world before the truth has a chance to get its pants on," has often been ascribed to British statesman Winston Churchill, a version of the phrase was coined by the satirical genius Jonathan Swift in 1710, who wrote, "Falsehood flies, and the Truth comes limping after it."

In 1855, London preacher Charles Haddon Spurgeon used it in a sermon:

> If you want truth to go round the world you must hire an express train to pull it; but if you want a lie to go round the world, it will fly; it is as light as a feather, and a breath will carry it. It is well said in the old Proverb, 'A lie will go round the world while truth is pulling its boots on.'[2]

Whether a lie is found out now or later, we can take comfort knowing that the Father in Heaven sees all and will judge accordingly. Meanwhile, we must counter lies and hate in the best possible way— with truth and grace.

## CHAPTER 1

# THE BIBLICAL VIEW
# OF HATE—AND LOVE

"**E**nough is enough!" With these words, Dr. Frank Wright, president of D. James Kennedy Ministries, threw down the gauntlet, becoming the first Christian ministry to challenge one of the nation's most prominent "civil rights" groups. The Southern Poverty Law Center (SPLC) was founded in the 1970's to combat the Ku Klux Klan and other white supremacists. In recent years, however, the SPLC has shifted its focus to what it calls the "radical right," targeting Christian organizations, which it labels "hate groups."

D. James Kennedy Ministries filed a lawsuit on August 23, 2017, after being included on the SPLC map of "all the active hate groups where you live," which appeared on CNN leading to the ministry being identified in local news reports as "the No. 1 hate group in Florida." Also named in the ministry's lawsuit was Amazon.com's charity program, AmazonSmile, which, based upon the SPLC designation of the organization as "anti-LGBT," excluded D. James Kennedy Ministries from participation as a designated nonprofit.

The ministry took out a full-page newspaper ad in which CEO Wright objected: "We do not hate anyone. We have been falsely branded by the SPLC for nothing more than subscribing to the teachings of the historic Christian faith." He added that those who knowingly label Christian ministries as "hate" groups solely for seeking to be faithful to the teachings of the Bible "are either woefully uninformed or willfully deceitful."

## "A New Commandment"

Most of us are familiar with slogans such as "Hate has no place in our society—we need to learn to love, not hate," or perhaps have seen lawn signs proclaiming, "Hate does not live here." Many people of faith instinctively agree with such expressions: they appear to mirror the commandment of Jesus to His disciples: "*A new command I give you: Love one another. As I have loved you, so you must love one another. By this everyone will know that you are my disciples, if you love one another*" (John 13:34-35).

The basis for love is none other than God Himself: "*We love because He first loved us. Whoever claims to love God yet hates a brother or sister is a liar. For whoever does not love their brother and sister, whom they have seen, cannot love God, whom they have not seen*" (1 John 4:19-20). We are warned of the dire consequences of hating others: "*Anyone who hates a brother or sister is a murderer, and you know that no murderer has eternal life residing in him*" (1 John 3:15). Inarguably, the Bible condemns holding personal animosity, bitterness, or resentment towards others.

## How Then Can a Loving God Be Said to "Hate" Certain People?

Yet, the Bible has much more to say about hate—the word appears more than 100 times in the Old and New Testaments. Many of these occurrences refer to "standing in opposition to" sin or to those who reject God. According to Merriam-Webster, the origin of the word goes back to the Old Goth *hatis* meaning "anger, enmity." The underlying sense of "rejecting evil" is found in passages such as: "*You love righteousness and hate wickedness; therefore God, your God, has set you above your companions by anointing you with the oil of joy*" (Psalm 45:7).

Throughout Scripture, the world we live in is portrayed as a battleground between God and the forces of evil, an ancient "enmity" that originated in the Garden of Eden, where the Lord cursed the devious Serpent: "*And I will put enmity between you and the woman, and between your offspring and hers; he will crush your head, and you will strike his heel*" (Genesis 3:15).

The "universalist" point of view insists that "God loves us so much that He will, in the end, save everyone." But this ignores the consequences of the original sin in the Garden, which the English writer G. K. Chesterton famously called "the one Christian doctrine that is empirically verifiable," having been abundantly validated by thousands of years of human history.

Despite the undeniable evidence of human suffering, violence, hardship and misery all around us, it has become increasingly fashionable to reject the reality of sin and evil. As evangelist Billy Graham once observed: "This generation is schooled in the teaching about an indulgent, soft-hearted God whose judgments are uncertain and who coddles those who break His commandments. This generation finds it difficult to believe that God hates sin."[1]

## Loving the Sinner while Hating the Sin

Love is at the heart of who God is, and what it means to be a Christian. Amazingly, while in one way or another each of us has rightfully earned the enmity of God, He continues to offer the possibility of forgiveness: "*But God demonstrates his own love for us in this: While we were still sinners, Christ died for us*" (Romans 5:8). Moreover, the offer of salvation is not withdrawn from anyone: "*The Lord is not slow in keeping his promise, as some understand slowness. Instead He is patient with you, not wanting anyone to perish, but everyone to come to repentance*" (2 Peter 3:9).

However, the undeniable reality is that the enemy of our very souls must be resisted with every fiber of our being. In the words of Jesus: "*The thief comes only to steal and kill and destroy; I have come that they may have life, and have it to the full*" (John 10:10).

Thus, when properly understood, it is incumbent upon all those who love God to "hate" that which stands in utter and contemptable opposition to Him, to truth, and to all that is good. That stance does not mean we are to hate individual sinners—again: "*while we were still sinners, Christ died for us.*" We, too, are sinners, justly deserving God's displeasure, yet we are saved by the grace of Him who loved us and loosed us from our sins by His own precious blood. Regrettably, it is one of the great deceptions of our day that believers who oppose evil and worship God—the very font of all love and goodness—are themselves maligned as "intolerant haters" who must by any and all means be suppressed.

## CHAPTER 2

# MISCASTING CHRISTIANS AND CHRISTIANITY

On February 1, 1993, a *Washington Post* front page article on conservative Christians contained this description of evangelicals: "largely poor, uneducated and easy to command."[1]

It caused a firestorm. Prompted by a clarion call from Pat Robertson on "The 700 Club" TV program, hundreds of Christians hit back with phone calls and emails to the *Post*.[2]

"They are very angry," said Joann Byrd, the *Post*'s ombudsman, whose job was to field complaints from the public. "People feel insulted. A lot of people have said, 'I am not poor, here's how much money I make. I am not uneducated, here are the graduate degrees I hold. And I do my own thinking.'"

Stung by the outburst, the *Post* quickly affixed a corrective statement that is still atop the article on the online version: "An article yesterday characterized followers of television evangelists Jerry Falwell and Pat Robertson as 'largely poor, uneducated and easy to command.' There is no factual basis for that statement."[3]

The reporter, Michael Weiskopf, later apologized, saying he made "an honest mistake, not born of any prejudice or malice for the religious right." He said his description was "overstated" and should have said evangelicals in general are "relatively" poor and uneducated.[4]

But how did it slide through so many editors?

Robert G. Kaiser, the *Post*'s managing editor, acknowledged a professional lapse as he and others failed to catch the "profoundly opinionated assertion" before publication. "We really screwed up. . . . One of the sins we commit from time to time is insensitivity."[5]

There's a reason for such "insensitivity"—a near absence of Bible-believing Christians in the nation's newsrooms, and a generally shared disdain among journalists for the Bible's clear directions on morality, particularly sexual morality.

Every so often a newspaper or broadcast outlet will do a story on a Christian-related topic such as a crisis pregnancy center or inner city ministry. While some reporters treat their subjects with respect, others report as if they are a National Geographic team exploring some exotic lost tribe in South America.

Someone once said that the opposite of love is not hate but indifference. Both are found in abundance in America's mass media.

Sometimes the ignorance appears to be an honest mistake, as when ABC anchorman Peter Jennings cited Second Chronicles as "Eleven Chronicles" in one of his segments. Another newsman misquoted the late Jerry Falwell as boasting of his "assault ministry." The Rev. Falwell had actually said "a salt ministry," a reference to Jesus' declaration urging Christians to be "salt and light" to their communities.

Sometimes, reporters air their own opinions by using amorphous identifiers, such as, "some say . . ." Or, "critics say that . . ." Or the old favorite, "sources say . . ."

Another way to inject opinion is to use an actual quote without any rebuttal. In an article about how Alabama voters viewed the controversy over allegations of sexual misconduct surrounding Alabama U.S. Senate candidate Roy Moore in November 2017, *Washington Post* reporters Elise Viebeck and Tom Hamburger included this from a woman who was protesting outside a Veterans Day breakfast that Moore, an outspoken Christian, addressed:

> "I'm not surprised," said Lisa Sharlach, 49, holding a sign that read "Grabby Old Pervert." "It's usually the people who are screaming God and Jesus that are the ones with skeletons in the closet."[6]

Ah, once again, the "Christians as hypocrites" theme so beloved in the newsroom. Does anyone honestly think that if the comment had been directed at, say, a Muslim, the slur would have stayed in the story?

## Hollywood's Cracked View of Christians

Once upon a time, movies portrayed Christians in a positive light. In "The Wizard of Oz" (1939), Dorothy's Auntie Em demonstrates Christian forbearance when she says that "as a Christian woman" she refuses to share out loud what she thinks of the mean woman who snatches away Dorothy's dog Toto. It's a minor scene in the classic film, but it speaks volumes about how Christianity's moral worldview was a given, even in Hollywood.

Think of the virtuous priests played by Bing Crosby in "Going My Way" (1944), "The Bells of St. Mary" (1945) and "Say One for Me" (1959). Pat O'Brien played a hero priest in "Angels with Dirty Faces" (1938) as did Spencer Tracy in "Boys Town" (1938).

When it was still respectful of Christianity, Hollywood also made a number of Biblical epics such as "The Robe" (1953), "The Ten Commandments" (1956,) "King of Kings" (1961), and "The Greatest Story Ever Told" (1965). In 2004, Mel Gibson's "The Passion of the Christ" was an outlier, surprising almost everyone by setting box office records worldwide.

In the Charlton Heston version of Ben-Hur (1959), Jesus makes several appearances, and in one of the most moving climactic scenes in cinematic history, his blood from the crucifixion heals Judah Ben-Hur's mother and sister of leprosy. In 2016, a new version of Ben-Hur was released to mixed reviews.

Beginning in the 1940s and picking up speed in the 1950s, the culture drifted toward moral relativism. By the 1960s, and especially in the late Sixties, Hollywood was awash in outright immorality, and Christians were increasingly cast as corrupt and villainous; or just plain narrow minded and ignorant. It didn't help that both the Catholic and Protestant film review boards closed their doors in 1965.

In the 1960 film "Inherit the Wind," Frederic March plays a character that is a stand-in for William Jennings Bryan, the creationist prosecutor in the famous Scopes monkey trial in Tennessee in 1925 in which a teacher, John Scopes, was convicted for teaching evolution. Playing the Clarence Darrow defense attorney role, Spencer Tracy utterly demolishes his opponent over his faith in the Bible's account of creation. Nominated for four Academy Awards, including Best Picture, "Inherit the Wind" is still listed frequently as one of the greatest films ever and is something of a celluloid "Bible" for secularists and atheists.

In 1982's Christopher Reeve vehicle "Monsignor," Catholic priests are at the heart of a financial scandal. The 1994 film "Priest" from Disney's Miramax studio, features an openly homosexual priest. Martin Scorsese's "The Last Temptation of Christ" (1988), went after Jesus Himself, portraying Him as having a sexual relationship with Mary Magdalene.

These are not merely exercises in artistic license, but frontal assaults on the very idea that some things are sacred and should not be trampled. There are countless other examples, such as the 1991 remake of "Cape Fear," in which Robert DeNiro plays a serial killer whose back is carved with Bible verses and who quotes Scripture just before raping and killing.

In "Misery" (1990), Kathy Bates won the Best Actress Oscar as a cross-wearing sadistic weirdo who tortures a prisoner for weeks. Film critic and talk show host Michael Medved wrote that this imagery was no accident:

> Perhaps in the hope of giving this slick and empty horror picture some deeper significance as a piece of social commentary, director Rob Reiner focuses repeatedly on the tiny gold cross that Ms. Bates wears around her neck; it often catches the light and flashes out at the camera, particularly on those occasions when her behavior is most menacing and bizarre.

In "The Shawshank Redemption" (1994), a powerful film from a Stephen King novel about two men in a tough prison finding friendship and hope, the villain is a Scripture-quoting, embezzling warden, who tells incoming inmates: "I believe in two things: discipline and the Bible. Here you'll receive both. Put your trust in the Lord; you're a-- belongs to me. Welcome to Shawshank."

More recently, the film and cable television adaptations of Margaret Atwood's dystopian novel "The Handmaid's Tale" portray a totalitarian future in which Scripture-spouting men lord it over women, forcing them to "breed" with them.

A steady flow of negative portrayals of a particular group can have a lasting impact on a culture. In fact, such propaganda can be downright dangerous if not countered. In the next section, we'll look at one of the most shocking examples.

## CHAPTER 3

# FROM RIDICULE TO GENOCIDE

During the 1930s, an entire nation—Germany—was harnessed by Adolf Hitler to hatred of a particular group, the Jews. Since it was one of the most educated nations in the world, many people wonder how Germany could have come under the sway of one of the most evil men in history.

It did not happen overnight. The seeds had been planted in the late 19th Century through the anti-Semitic rantings of the composer Richard Wagner and the writings of philosopher Friedrich Nietzsche, both of whom were instrumental in the formation of a young Adolf Hitler's worldview.[1]

In 1899, an Englishman-turned-German named H.S. Chamberlain published a sweeping, 1,200-page historical tome *Foundations of the Nineteenth Century*.[2] The best-selling book made the case that history's only meaningful element was race. The Germans, he wrote, would rise as a superior race and dominate the world. As for the Jews, they were another "pure" race, but whose blood should not be mixed with that of the "pure" Aryan blood of Germans. The book was an instant hit in Germany, selling 100,000 copies by the time World War I broke out in 1914. After the war, it climbed the charts again, with a 24th printing in 1938.[3]

Chamberlain, who died in 1927, proclaimed Jesus Christ as a major influence on humanity, but insisted that He could not have been Jewish. In fact, he wrote, "Whoever claimed that Jesus was a Jew was either being stupid or telling a lie . . . Jesus was not a Jew."[4]

William L. Shirer, author of *The Rise and Fall of the Third Reich: A History of Nazi Germany*, wrote that Chamberlain "was given to seeing demons who, by his own account, drove him on relentlessly. . . ."[5] His books were "written in the grip of a terrible fever, a veritable trance, a state of self-induced intoxication, so that, as he says in this autobiography, *Lebensweger*, he was often unable to recognize them as his own work."[6] Chamberlain became a folk hero, and "his racial theories and his burning sense of the destiny of the Germans and Germany were taken over by the Nazis, who acclaimed him as one of their prophets . . . extolling the 'spiritual founder' of National Socialist Germany."[7]

Driven by the theory of racial superiority, the National Socialist German Workers Party rose under Adolf Hitler. At the same time, the country's Jewish population was subjected first to ridicule, then character assassination, and finally to persecution that led to the Holocaust. Jews had obtained prominent positions throughout German society, so the initial negative portrayals did not overly alarm them. They thought the disturbing newspaper imagery was a temporary phenomenon.

## Anti-Semitic Literature Is Commissioned

As they consolidated power, the Nazi regime began commissioning openly anti-Semitic films and books.

A children's book, *Der Giftpilz* (The Poisonous Mushroom), published in 1938 by the notorious anti-Semite Julius Streicher, compares Jews to dangerous fungi that are difficult to tell from wholesome mushrooms (gentiles).[8] It was only one of many such books distributed in German schools.[9]

One of the most infamous vehicles was "The Eternal Jew," a 1940 film that compared Jews to "swarms of rats that are going to take over cities if left unchecked." Jews are also described as the "demon behind the corruption of mankind."[10] By 1941, the film "Heimkehr" depicted the Jews as prompting Polish people to commit atrocities against the German minority in that country.[11]

Soon, the portrayals became even more vicious as the Nazi Party's artists, cartoonists and filmmakers began demonizing the

Jews: "The Greedy Jew," "The Sadistic Jew," and "The Molester Jew" became staples in the nation's media until the Jews became identified as a threat to Germany's moral and fiscal health. Building on this relentlessly negative campaign against the Jews, Hitler was able to enact laws banning Jews from owning newspapers, publishing houses, and radio and film studios or to teach at universities or work in any profession where values are transmitted.[12]

By 1938, the Nazis were beginning to subject the Jews to extreme violence. On November 9th and 10th of that year, in a massive outburst of murder, vandalism, and rape, thousands of Jewish shops, synagogues, homes, and other Jewish-identified places were attacked, and 20,000 Jews arrested. Thirty-six deaths—all of Jews—were reported.[13] The awful event was dubbed Kristallnacht (night of crystal, or broken glass).[14]

In the ensuing years, the Nazis rounded up not only Germany's Jews but those in captured nations such as Poland and France. Estimates vary for Hitler's "Final Solution" to the Jews, but the Holocaust Museum and other authorities put the number of Jews killed in concentration camps at six million.

Less often acknowledged is Hitler's hatred of Christianity and his persecution of churches that resisted his power. Thousands of Catholic priests and Protestant pastors were rounded up and sent to the concentration camps, where most died of disease or starvation or were executed.[15] At first, Hitler seduced willing clerics into supporting his regime. But dissidents were soon ferreted out and harshly treated. The Nazis created a National Reich Church, among whose tenets was a demand for "immediate cessation of the publishing and dissemination of the Bible in Germany."[16]

One of the most famous sayings to emerge from this era came from Pastor Martin Niemöller, who had supported Hitler initially but went into opposition and was imprisoned in 1937 after he realized the Fuehrer's evil intent. In post-war lectures, he would tell his audience:

*First they came for the Socialists, and I did not speak out—*

*Because I was not a Socialist.*
*Then they came for the Trade Unionists, and I did not speak out—*
*Because I was not a Trade Unionist.*
*Then they came for the Jews, and I did not speak out—*
*Because I was not a Jew.*
*Then they came for me—and there was no one left to speak for me.*[17]

History offers other tragic examples of groups that were similarly demonized.

In Mao Tse Tung's China, during the decade-long Cultural Revolution that began in 1966, intellectuals were mocked and pilloried before being sent to concentration camps, where many were executed. In communist Cambodia in the 1970s, the regime rounded up anyone who wore glasses, because they presumed they could read and, thus, be counter witnesses to the regime's propaganda.

Even America has experienced periods in which some groups have been debased. Native Americans and Chinese immigrants were subjected to absurdly comic or demeaning portrayals. During the Jim Crow era following Reconstruction and right up until the passage of the Civil Rights Act of 1964, black Americans were treated as second-class citizens and were so demeaned in the American South that it prompted lynchings.[18]

During wartime, it is common for nations to depict their enemies as less than human. In World War II, the Axis powers routinely cast American G.I.s as baby killers, while American posters depicted Japanese as buck-toothed barbarians. The point of all such propaganda is to deny the enemy's humanity.

On a far lesser scale, the steady flow of negative imagery of Christians is corroding respect for Christianity and for the rights of Christians to act on their beliefs. If Christians are simply "haters," and society has a duty to wipe out hate, Christians wind up in the bulls-eye of such efforts.

## CHAPTER 4

# HATE CRIMES: WHAT WERE YOU THINKING?

Thanks to America's Founders, we have had a tradition of free speech ever since passage of the Bill of Rights in 1791. The First Amendment has been a bulwark against quashing public expression of ideas. Although blatantly misused in recent years to shield non-speech like pornography, the First Amendment has functioned as a remarkably powerful device for protecting basic freedoms.

Frontal assaults on the First Amendment have been largely ineffective, with some notable exceptions, such as the "bubble" law that prohibits pro-life protestors within a certain distance from abortion clinics.

More recently, Christians are being told to keep their beliefs out of the public square in the name of stamping out "hate." An ideological end-run is underway that could prove to be the greatest general threat to First Amendment freedoms in American history: so-called hate crime laws, and related policies in the public and private sectors. Christians, in particular, need to pay attention because there is a campaign underway to reframe Biblical morality as actionable "hate speech."

"Hate crime" laws do something that American law is not supposed to do: they get into a person's head. American legal tradition holds that government may regulate people's actions, but not their beliefs or thoughts. To do otherwise would be to violate the conscience and to chill the related First Amendment freedoms of speech, religion, press, and assembly. Totalitarian and authoritarian governments routinely violate the conscience by abridging these rights, which Americans take for granted.

At first blush, so-called hate crime laws sound like a good thing. We don't want anyone attacked just for having a personal or group identity that someone finds offensive. When Jim Crow laws were in force following the Civil War and right up to the Civil Rights Act of 1964, the law itself was rigged in Southern states to openly discriminate against black Americans. Today, however, the memory of that shocking legacy is being misused to create new civil rights claims that threaten freedom of conscience.

## Hate Crime Policies Are Advancing

Hate crime policies are advancing in America through speech codes on college campuses; local, state and federal laws; growing self-censorship in the culture; corporate policies; and international pressure.

Here's a basic definition from a Massachusetts commission:

> A "hate crime" is a crime in which the perpetrator's conduct is motivated, in whole or in part, by hatred, bias, or prejudice, based on the actual or perceived race, color, religion, national origin, gender, disability, or sexual orientation of another group or individual.
>
> Hate crimes are characterized by bias indicators: "objective facts, circumstances or patterns attending a criminal act(s) which, standing alone or in conjunction with other facts and circumstances, suggest that an offender's actions were motivated, in whole or in part, by any [prohibited] form of bias . . ." The most common bias indicators are verbal slurs, epithets, and bigoted language, written or spoken. Careful attention to bias indicator evidence is essential to appropriate investigation and charging of these offenses.[1]

Although the term "hate crime" is being tossed around indiscriminately as a form of name-calling, hate crimes laws themselves increase the penalty that applies to crimes of violence, threats and harassment, and property damage whenever a prohibited bias motive is proven. For example, the penalty applicable to a simple assault and battery, which causes even minor injury to its victim, rises with a hate crime charge from a mere two and one-half years to as much as seventeen and one-half years of incarceration. Hate-motivated activity also exposes perpetrators to the risk of being subjected to a civil rights injunction.

Each year, the FBI collects data on hate crimes from state police agencies, with nearly 17,000 currently reporting. As a category, actual hate crimes are almost microscopic. For instance, in 2016, there were 1.2 million violent crimes, including 17,250 murders and 95,730 rapes. Nearly 8 million property crimes were also reported.[2] Hate crimes totaled 7,121.[3] That still might sound like a lot, and it is certainly traumatic in each individual case for the victims, but the United States population is more than 325 million people.[4]

Of single-bias incidents, 57.5 percent were motivated by a race/ethnicity/ancestry bias; 21 percent by religious bias; 17.7 percent from sexual-orientation bias; 2.0 percent by gender-identity bias; 1.2 percent from disability bias, and 0.5 percent (31 incidents) gender bias.

All of these statistics need to be taken with a grain of salt, since reporting varies from state to state, and several states and some large cities do not even file reports.[5] Some hate crimes, such as vandalism against a church, synagogue, or mosque, which affect numerous people, are counted as a single property crime.

But despite an onslaught of media headlines, America is not awash in hate crimes. Part of the media's fascination stems from the belief of many liberal reporters that America is deeply and uniquely racist or homophobic, and the public needs to be reminded of this as often as possible.

## Support for Hate Crime Laws

One of America's greatest assets is its heritage of protecting the downtrodden. Although laws are not always evenly applied, and life is not fair, Americans feel that everyone is entitled to a measure of dignity, and if need be, his or her day in court. Hate crime proponents benefit from the American public's inherent desire to "play fair." When they talk of combating hate, they strike a chord in the American heart, and it speaks well of us as a people.

The Western notion that every life is precious flows from the Bible's declaration that humans are made in God's image. Therefore, each individual's life and dignity are worth defending. The Declaration of Independence proclaims "that all men are created equal, that they are endowed by their Creator with certain unalienable Rights."

Just as important to our vision of ordered liberty is the concept that man is imperfect and capable of making mistakes. That is why America's Founders created a system of limited government. If men are flawed, they reasoned, then no person or group should have ultimate control over fellow citizens.

The gap between the Biblical admonition of the Golden Rule ("do unto others as you would have them do unto you") and the injustice of slavery eventually sparked America's greatest and bloodiest conflict, an end to the buying and selling of human beings, and the beginning of the civil rights movement. But along the way, the notion of protecting our civil rights from government morphed into a campaign for government to acquire many more powers in order to correct lingering injustices.

## Inventing New Categories

As a result, government grew at all levels, with the federal government growing most of all. The civil rights movement, having won virtually every battle to establish equality under the law, began a quest to create an ever growing list of new victims, particularly categories based on sexual behavior.

Unlike skin color or ethnicity, however, which cannot change and have no moral component, sexual behavior is volitional, changeable, and is deeply imbued with moral value. By equating sexual behavior with skin color, activists have hijacked the moral capital of the black civil rights movement and bent it to their goal of criminalizing Christian morality.

When disapproval of homosexuality, bisexuality, or transgenderism is equated with racism, the result is that the civil rights enforcement machine, including government agencies, media, schools, and corporate human resource departments, begin enforcing anti-discrimination laws and policies that were designed for an entirely different purpose.

This puts Christians in the bulls-eye, as we will see in the next chapter. "Hate crime" law and policies take us far beyond the "equality" wars and into a truly Orwellian realm of authority. They take us into mind reading and belief assessment.

Proponents of hate crime laws insist that they deter hate-related violence, and that they have nothing to do with thoughts or beliefs. But this is absurd. Standard criminal law already punishes murder, theft, burglary, kidnapping, perjury, etc. A hate crime sentencing enhancement, therefore, deals only with the beliefs of the perpetrator, taking the law into a previously forbidden area—the human heart. In effect, a defendant is first convicted of a crime, then convicted of a criminal thought. Depending on the perpetrator's or victim's identity, this opens the door to selective enforcement.

For centuries, the law has properly stayed out of the realm of the human heart for good reason: The heart is unfathomable. According to the prophet Jeremiah, we don't even know our own hearts: *"The heart is deceitful above all things, and desperately wicked. Who can know it?"* (Jeremiah 17:9 NKJV). Therefore, how can we expect other human beings to read our hearts with enough precision to impose a lengthier prison sentence?

In the Sermon on the Mount, Jesus advised His followers, *"Judge not, that you be not judged"* (Matthew 7:1 NKJV). Although this directive has been taken wildly out of context to justify virtually every departure from moral norms, Jesus is talking about the human heart, not actions.

The Golden Rule includes acknowledging that we are not capable of reading someone else's heart with certainty any more than other people can read ours. Elsewhere in the Gospels, Jesus condemns wrongful behavior itself in no uncertain terms.

Earlier generations knew that when you presumed to know someone else's heart, you were usurping an ability unique to the Divine. There are terms describing this in the Bible itself (blasphemy), and also in modern psychiatric literature (megalomania).

On a more worldly plain, the threat of hate crime laws and policies is that they put the citizen on the couch (or behind bars), while attempting to answer the question: "What were you thinking?"

# Racial Hatred Is No Match for God's Love

*In this excerpt from a July 2017 column, "Jesus Is the Answer for Our Racial Divide," D. James Kennedy Ministries Senior On-Air Producer Jerry Newcombe tells why the Christian message is one of healing, not hate.*

What is the ultimate solution to the racial divide in America? Jesus, because in Christ, there is no black or white—we are one—when we are in Christ.

One time I interviewed for Christian TV a former racist, who had been with a violent wing of the Ku Klux Klan.

His name is Tommy Tarrants, Jr., a native of Mobile, Alabama. The FBI agent trailing him called him a "mad dog killer."

After a shoot-out in Mississippi, Tarrants was arrested, and the November 28, 1968, newspaper headline read: "Tarrants Found Guilty, Sentenced to 30 Years."

The story reported, "A self-styled guerrilla waging a 'holy crusade' against a 'Communist-Jewish conspiracy' was convicted Wednesday night of the attempted bombing of the home of a Jewish businessman."

But even this man, blinded as he was by racism, bigotry, and hate, found the truth in a life- changing encounter with Jesus who can shatter racism and every other –ism in the human heart.

While Tommy read the Bible in prison, God removed the scales from his eyes. He said, "I got on my knees in that cell and just gave my life completely to Christ . . . I said, 'Lord, I've ruined my life, but if you want it, I'll just give it to you completely. Here it is.' And something changed inside of me when I did that, I could even feel it. Something happened and I became different."

Tarrants was eventually released and got involved in ministry in the D.C. area, including as a pastor of an inter-racial church. Tarrants even wrote a book with John Perkins, a black evangelical minister who had been beaten during the Civil Rights days. The book is called, *He's My Brother.*

Dr. King's vision of a color-blind society, where people are judged not by the color of their skin, but by the content of their character, is a great ideal to strive for. The change of the human heart—which can happen in Christ—is what can ultimately solve America's racial divide.

## CHAPTER 5

# DEPLOYING HATE AS A POLITICAL WEAPON

In June 2017, self-avowed Democratic Socialist Sen. Bernie Sanders of Vermont questioned the fitness of Wheaton College alumnus Russell Vought for the post of deputy director of the Office of Management and Budget at his confirmation hearing. Mr. Vought had written an article in which he said that Muslims "do not know God because they have rejected Jesus Christ his Son, and they stand condemned."

This is basic Christian theology, and it applies to everyone, not just Muslims. Jesus Himself said, "*I am the Way, the Truth and the Life. No one comes to the Father except through me*" (John 14:6).

Sen. Sanders accused Mr. Vought of religious bigotry, saying, "In my view, the statement made by Mr. Vought is indefensible, it is hateful, it is Islamophobic, and it is an insult to over a billion Muslims throughout the world."

How about the billion Christians that Sen. Sanders just equated with bigots?

The very next week, progressive lawmakers showed more disdain for Christians during the hearing for President Trump's Seventh Circuit Court of Appeals nominee, Amy Coney Barrett, a devout Catholic and Notre Dame law professor.

"Whatever a religion is, it has its own dogma," said Sen. Dianne Feinstein (D-Calif.). "The law is totally different. And I think in your case, professor, when you read your speeches, the conclusion one draws is that the dogma lives loudly within you, and that's of concern when you come to big issues that large numbers of people have fought for for years in this country."

Sen. Feinstein's message was that only nominal believers or

non-believers are suited for public office, and that if someone takes Christianity seriously, that puts them out of the running.

Sen. Dick Durbin (D-Ill.) asked Ms. Barrett, "Do you consider yourself an orthodox Catholic?" He stopped just short of the McCarthyesque query, "Are you now or have you ever been a member of the Catholic Church?"

Former Sen. Al Franken (D-Min.) tossed guilt by association into the mix by condemning the nominee for speaking before a "hate" group. The organization being maligned was the Alliance Defending Freedom (ADF), a Christian attorneys group among whose founders was Dr. D. James Kennedy. ADF litigates religious freedom cases all over the country, including the case of cake-maker Jack Phillips, which was argued before the Supreme Court in December 2017.

The absurd "hate" designation for ADF came courtesy of a truly hate-filled group, the Southern Poverty Law Center (SPLC), an Alabama-based leftist legal outfit that lumps mainstream Christian organizations in with violent extremist groups such as the Ku Klux Klan and skinheads. (For a fuller picture, see Chapter Seven.)

## Fewer Christians, More Attacks

There are troubling signs that the United States is entering a post-Christian era. According to the Pew Research Center, from 2007 to 2014 the percentage of Americans who are "absolutely certain" that God exists fell from 71 percent to 63 percent.[1]

This is a sharp drop from earlier polls, which as late as the early 1990s indicated that between 94 percent and 98 percent of the American public believed in "God or a universal spirit."[2] Shockingly, the most recent Pew Research poll shows that only 18 percent of those between the ages of 18-29 have a strong belief in the existence of God.

The decline in the numbers of active Christians has prompted concerns that religious expression is under attack.

"This new vigorous secularism has catapulted mockery of Christianity and other forms of religious traditionalism into the mainstream and set a new low for what counts as civil criticism of people's most-cherished beliefs," writes scholar and social critic Mary Eberstadt. "The 'faith of our fathers' is controversial as never before."[3]

## Words Have Consequences

On August 12, 2012, 29-year-old Floyd Lee Corkins II entered the headquarters of the Family Research Council (FRC) holding a gun and carrying a backpack filled with Chick-fil-A sandwiches—which symbolized the reason why Corkins was targeting FRC. The chicken sandwich restaurant chain had been a vocal supporter of traditional marriage, which the Christian organization had long championed.[4] The attack was thwarted when the unarmed building manager, Leo Johnson, who had been shot in the arm by Corkins, was able to disarm and restrain him.

What could have motivated such a potentially horrific murder spree? Two years earlier, the Southern Poverty Law Center (SPLC) designated FRC as a "hate group" because of their support for traditional marriage. During his interrogation, Corkins cited the SPLC's "hate list" as the reason why he decided to attack FRC: "Southern Poverty Law lists anti-gay groups. I found them online, did a little research, went to the website, stuff like that." He would later admit in court that he hoped to "kill as many as possible and smear the Chick-Fil-A sandwiches in victims' faces, and kill the guard."[5]

Corkins was sentenced to 25 years on attempted murder and terrorism charges.[6] He was the first person convicted under the District of Columbia's anti-terrorism law.[7]

The Southern Poverty Law Center, however, still identifies FRC and many other Christian organizations as "anti-gay" hate groups on its "hate map." FRC President Tony Perkins stated that "The SPLC's reckless labeling has led to devastating consequences. Because of its 'hate group' lists, a deadly terrorist had a guide map to FRC and other organizations. Our staff is still reeling from the attack, and the chilling effect this could have on organizations that are simply fighting for their values is outrageous."[8]

## Faith in the Crosshairs

Tragically, the attempted mass shooting at FRC is not an isolated incident, but rather the beginning of a disturbing trend of violent attacks against Christians. On October 1, 2015, Christopher Harper-Mercer, 26, opened fire at Umpqua Community College in Roseburg, Oregon, killing 10 and wounding seven before turning his gun on himself. Student Stacy Boylan relates that as he reloaded his gun, Harper-Mercer demanded to know who among the students were Christians: "And they would stand up, and he said, 'Good, because you're a Christian, you're going to see God in just about one second.' What happened then was a merciless slaughter: And then he shot and killed them."[9]

The peacefulness of a rural Texas Sunday morning was shattered on November 5, 2017, when Devin Patrick Kelley, 26, stormed into the First Baptist Church in Sutherland Springs, committing the deadliest attack on a church in American history. Clad in black and wearing a ballistic vest, Kelley opened fire with a military-style rifle, killing many of the parishioners. Within minutes, 26 people aged 5 to 72 lay dead or dying, with scores wounded before Kelley fled and later died. Former classmates described him as "an outcast and atheist who used social media to mock Christianity."[10] As *Washington Times* writer Cheryl K. Chumley wryly notes: "Too bad for the mainstream media, which no doubt would've loved to make the case that Kelley was a card-carrying Christian, a Bible-thumping Republican, a tea party type conservative to the core."[11]

## Intolerance by Any Other Name

Antifa—short for anti-fascist action—burst on the national scene in the wake of the 2016 presidential election, spurred to action by what they perceived as the dangerously right-wing Trump administration. The moniker stands for a loose coalition of radical leftist groups and individuals, many of which identify as anarchists who claim to oppose white nationalist groups, racists, and neo-Nazis. Up until the rise of the movement, non-violent protest was a time-honored tradition across much of the political spectrum. No longer. A defining characteristic of Antifa is that they unapologetically claim to oppose fascism "by any means necessary."

Antifa activists have become "increasingly confrontational and dangerous, so much so that the Department of Homeland Security formally classified their activities as 'domestic terrorist violence.'"[12] According to intelligence documents obtained by *Politico*, "These Antifa guys were showing up with weapons, shields and bike helmets and just beating the s*** out of people. . . . They're using Molotov cocktails, they're starting fires, they're throwing bombs and smashing windows." *Politico* reported that photos show Antifa "brandishing ax handles and shields, often with industrial-sized bolts attached to create crude bayonets. A senior state law enforcement official said, 'A whole bunch of them' have been deemed dangerous enough to be placed on U.S. terrorism watch lists."[13]

Of particular concern to conservative Christians is the fact that Antifa explicitly identifies "homophobia" and "sexism" as fascist "hate speech" that they are sworn to oppose. According to one Antifa sympathizer: "Some religious beliefs, sincerely held, are detestable. They cannot be spoken without disrupting social peace."[14] The growing trend to stigmatize those who hold to conservative social issues—and to justify attacking what they consider "fascist hate speech" by "any means necessary"—threatens to unleash a new era of oppression upon people of faith.

CHAPTER 6

# THE RISE OF
# CULTURAL MARXISM

After the Russian Revolution of 1917, when communists under Vladimir Lenin seized power and soon created what would become the atheistic Soviet Union of Socialist Republics, Marxist leaders and thinkers expected the rest of the world to experience economic upheaval. When it did not happen, some Marxists realized that it would take more than a revolt by factory laborers and farm workers led by an elite "vanguard of the proletariat"—it would require a cultural revolution.

Christianity and the free market system were so deeply entrenched in Europe and America that only a massive change in cultural values could produce the conditions conducive to a socialist political and economic revolution grounded in rejection of God. Antonio Gramsci (1891-1937), an Italian communist, called on his fellow revolutionaries to "capture the culture" by taking over the societal institutions that transmit cultural values—schools, the arts, the media, community organizations, even the church.[1]

In pre-war Germany, as the Nazis began rounding up their enemies, intellectuals from the leftist Frankfurt School for Social Research fled to Geneva, Switzerland, and then the United States, where they worked to infiltrate cultural institutions and bend them to their collectivist vision.[2]

One of the Frankfurt School's refugees was Herbert Marcuse, who wrote *Eros and Civilization* in 1955. The book was a manifesto for changing social values through the embrace of sex and the sensual. In one sense, this was not a new approach; leftists had been preaching against sexual morality since the mid-19th Century. They rightly saw sexual fidelity as the foundation of marriage, and marriage the foundation of the family, and the family as an obstacle in the way of ceding all power to the state.[3] Marcuse's book found itching ears on American campuses, and helped give an intellectual excuse for the abandonment of morality in the name of liberation.

## "Hate Speech" Must Be Silenced

Along with promoting sexual immorality as a freedom-granting elixir, the cultural Marxists campaigned to suppress opinions other than their own. Given the climate on many campuses today, they have succeeded beyond their wildest dreams. Certain opinions and views, especially those that reflect Biblical morality, are considered so "toxic" that they now constitute "hate speech."

The Marxist-inspired war on free speech is the fountain of what has come to be known as "political correctness," or PC. Any defense of Christianity or even Western civilization is considered politically incorrect "hate speech" that must be silenced. America and the West, having sprung from Christendom, are seen as the major cause of the world's problems, and should be regarded only as "oppressors." On the other hand, virtually any culture other than Western culture is accorded respect under the doctrine of multiculturalism, which says that no system is any better than any other—except that the West is evil.

It is a little like the inherent inconsistency in radical feminism, another philosophy that rests on falsehoods about human nature. Radical feminists insist that men and women are identical and interchangeable in all ways, except that women are superior. If you instead believe that God created male and female as distinctively different and complementary, you are an "oppressor."

Under PC, it is not enough to remain silent in the face of the Left's radical transformation of social values. Everyone must submit or else.

On many campuses, students can file formal complaints if their professors fail to give them "trigger warnings" to indicate that they might hear views that offend them or hurt their feelings. This could be something as seemingly innocent as using the terms "husbands" or "wives."

Many "diversity" policies have provisions for re-education sessions, which are supposed to elevate offenders into an enlightened way of thinking. They must recant and even voice their acceptance of the new order of multicultural, racial, sexual, or ethical diversity.

## The PC Web

Caught in the PC web are Christians who are trying to live out their faith, which is becoming increasingly difficult as cultural Marxism takes hold.

At the University of California's Hastings College of Law, for example, the campus chapter of the Christian Legal Society was denied official recognition in 2009 because it requires leaders to sign a "Statement of Faith" and excludes those who engage in "unrepentant homosexual conduct."[4] In other words, to be leaders of a Christian club they have to be Christians who believe in the deity of Jesus Christ and agree to live according to Biblical sexual morality.

This was too much for the school, which accused the club of discrimination. In a 5-4 ruling on June 10, 2010, the U.S. Supreme Court rejected the Christian club's straightforward First Amendment-based appeal. The opinion, written by Justice Ruth Bader Ginsburg, a former ACLU attorney, said the school's "all comers policy" is a "reasonable viewpoint-neutral condition."

In California, beginning in 2018, health care workers who address a senior transgender patient with the "wrong" pronouns (in other words, the ones that indicate their birth sex) may face up to one year in jail—a harsher penalty than for people who knowingly infect others with HIV.[5] California Gov. Jerry Brown signed the legislation in October 2017, along with another bill lowering the maximum penalty for knowingly infecting or exposing a person to HIV to six months in prison—down from a maximum of eight years.[6]

## Cultural Marxism's Ultimate Tactic

The ultimate tactic of cultural Marxism is to redefine traditional moral values and even expression of biological truth as a form of "hate" punishable by law. Under such a system, common sense is banished and the state forces people to lie.

In his novel *1984*, George Orwell vividly illustrates the nightmare that ensues when a totalitarian government, aided by modern methods, exceeds its legitimate reach and delves into the human soul. Although Orwell's protagonist, Winston, has already agreed to comply with all the laws and rules, his relentless interrogator informs him that he is not quite there:

> "Tell me, what are your feelings about Big Brother?"
> "I hate him."
> "You hate him. Good. Then the time has come for you to take the last step. You must love Big Brother. It is not enough to obey him; you must love him."[7]

The good news, as always, is that such evil has an end-date, whereas God's love is for all of eternity.

As Fulton Sheen once remarked crisply, "Take heart that Christ's tomb is empty, while Lenin's tomb is not."

# Rules for Radicals

Today's radical movements thrive by dividing people into identity groups and teaching them to hate America, middle-class Americans, and especially conservative Christians. Much of the genesis of this strategy can be traced to labor activist Saul Alinsky. Alinsky wrote two extremely influential books— *Reveille for Radicals* (1945) and the better known *Rules for Radicals* (1971).

The latter book, which is packed with practical political tactics, has become the virtual Bible of leftwing politics.[1] In her 1969 thesis at Wellesley College, "There Is Only The Fight," Hillary Rodham (later Hillary Rodham Clinton) lionized Alinsky.[2] And Barack Obama studied under Alinsky's protégés while working as an activist lawyer in Chicago.[3]

Anyone wondering why this primer on "community organizing" is so devilishly clever might want to read Alinsky's dedication for *Rules for Radicals*: To "the first radical known to man who rebelled against the establishment and did it so effectively that he at least won his own kingdom—Lucifer."

Alinsky referred to ordinary, decent Americans as "the enemy."

"Teaching hatred for the normal majority is the key to power for radicals," wrote James Lewis in *American Thinker*.

> But Alinsky taught that you can't easily hate millions of people. To do that effectively you need a one-person scapegoat to focus all your hatred on. 'Pick the target, freeze it, personalize it, and polarize it.'[4] That is the politics of personal destruction, and it doesn't matter if the target is black like Clarence Thomas, or a woman like Sarah Palin, or a severely wounded war veteran like John McCain.[5]

This helps explain the extraordinary vitriol aimed at President Trump by every faction on the Left—including the so-called mainstream media. It is calculated to destroy his presidency, not merely oppose it.

Another Alinsky mantra is: "Make the enemy live up to their own book of rules."[6] No one can possibly live up to the ideal, so radicals quote Scripture selectively to make Christians out to be hypocrites. "No organization, including organized religion, can live up to the letter of its own book. You can club them to death with their book of rules and regulations."[7]

Alinsky's fourth principle is summarized this way: "*Ridicule is man's most potent weapon.* It is almost impossible to counterattack ridicule." Hence, the relentless nasty jokes from leftwing celebrities that make Christians out to be objects of ridicule.

If there were any doubt as to which side is stirring up hostility, Alinsky makes it clear: "To the questioner nothing is sacred. He detests dogma, defies any finite definition of morality, rebels against any repression of a free, open search for ideas no matter where they may lead. He is challenging, insulting, agitating, discrediting. He stirs unrest."[8]

Finally, Alinsky and his disciples count on Christians and other opponents to react in kind. "The real action is the enemy's reaction. The enemy properly goaded and guided in his reaction will be your major strength."[9]

All the more reason to take to heart Jesus' admonition to rise above provocation and love them: "*But I say to you who hear, Love your enemies, do good to those who hate you*" (Luke 6:27 ESV).

## CHAPTER 7

# THE SPLC:
# TRADING IN HATE WHILE
# POINTING A FINGER

*"When the Christian faith is treated as a menace and its
influence is screened out of our public life, with it goes the
virtues that are necessary for a nation to remain free."*
– Dr. D. James Kennedy

One day in February 2015, the famed neurosurgeon and outspoken Christian author Dr. Ben Carson woke up to find himself listed as an "extremist" on a nationally known "hate list."[1] Neither he nor his many admirers could believe what they were seeing. The "extremist" designation was the work of the Southern Poverty Law Center (SPLC), which once did some good work tracking genuine hate groups such as neo-Nazis and the Ku Klux Klan, but has morphed in recent years into perhaps the most virulently hateful anti-Christian group in America.

After a widespread outcry, the SPLC de-listed Dr. Carson, who later ran for the Republican nomination for president. But the SPLC continues to list several of Dr. Carson's statements that they regard as "extremist," most notably his support for God's first human institution, marriage.

Responding in a Facebook post, Dr. Carson wrote:

> When embracing traditional Christian values is equated to hatred, we are approaching the stage where wrong is called right and right is called wrong. It is important for us to once again advocate true tolerance.

That means being respectful of those with whom we disagree and allowing people to live according to their values without harassment. It is nothing but projectionism when some groups label those who disagree with them as haters.[2]

The SPLC, which was co-founded in 1971 by direct-mail marketing whiz Morris Dees, collects tens of millions of dollars each year via direct mail by issuing dire warnings that now-tiny hate groups like the Klan are taking over America. With an endowment of more than $315 million, the SPLC stashes millions in cash in overseas accounts.[3]

In a brief history of the SPLC for *RealClearPolitics*, Carl Cannon wrote:

> For the past 47 years, Morris Dees has been selling fear and hate.
>
> The business model is simple, albeit cynical, and best illustrated by its most famous case. In 1987, a Dees-led legal team won a $7 million judgment against the Ku Klux Klan in a wrongful death suit on behalf of Beulah Mae Donald, the mother of a 19-year-old kid murdered by members of the racist group. But the defendants' total assets amounted to a building worth $52,000. That's how much Mrs. Donald, who died the following year, received. But Dees reaped $9 million for the SPLC from fundraising solicitations about the case, including one showing a grisly photo of Michael Donald's corpse.[4]

## A New List of "Haters"

The SPLC's current long list of "haters" includes many prominent individuals, such as psychologist and Focus on the Family founder Dr. James Dobson, and smears anyone opposing its increasingly radical sexual agenda.

On its website, SPLC maintains a "hate map" containing the names and addresses of "hate groups" all over the country.[5] Recent imagery includes a man giving a Nazi salute and people waving Confederate flags. Listed are mainstream Christian organizations, including D. James Kennedy Ministries (DJKM), the American Family Association, Alliance Defending Freedom, and many others. All of them have been lumped in with truly racist and violent groups merely because the Christian groups espouse Biblical sexual morality, including the belief that God created marriage only as the union of one man and one woman.

Other groups and individuals are listed because they oppose radical Islam, abortion on demand, or favor enforcing federal immigration laws. Radio hosts Rush Limbaugh, Glenn Beck, Michael Savage and Sandy Rios are named, along with columnists Ann Coulter, Laura Ingraham (now a Fox News show host), Pat Buchanan and Fox News' Lou Dobbs and Sean Hannity, and conservative groups such as the Constitution Party, Tea Party Patriots, and the Center for Security Policy.

Because the SPLC has cast such a wide net, unwarranted inclusion on their hate list has become something of a badge of honor, even though most "honorees" would rather the SPLC cease defaming them.

## Far-Reaching Consequences

The mere presence on the SPLC's hate map has demonstrably far-reaching consequences, as we have already seen in the attempted mass murder at the Family Research Council in August 2012 by a troubled young man who had bought into the SPLC's hate message, something the group's leaders refuse to correct.

In a full-page ad in the *Washington Post* in June 2017, the SPLC explained why, despite the clear link to a terrorist attack, it continued to list the Family Research Council on its online "hate map." They quoted from FRC statements that warn that homosexuality is "unnatural," has "negative physical and psychological health effects," and is being peddled to children. They don't try to refute any of this—because they can't.

March 2017, a speech by American Enterprise Institute scholar Charles Murray at Vermont's Middlebury College had to be moved because of threats of violence from protesters who alleged that Murray was a "white supremacist." During the transition, a mob assaulted and injured political science Prof. Allison Stanger, sending her to the hospital. In her account, she said, "I feared for my life."[6] Later, some of the attackers cited the SPLC's labeling of Murray as a "racist" to justify the violence.

On June 14, 2017, Bernie Sanders follower James T. Hodgkinson, who had "liked" the SPLC on Facebook, shot up Republican congressmen and their staffs at a baseball practice in Alexandria, Virginia, critically wounding Republican Majority Whip Steve Scalise, and injuring four others. The Louisiana congressman had been singled out by the SPLC for an alleged connection to a white power group, a charge he has denied.[7]

## GuideStar Compromises Its "Neutrality"

Another major harm done by the SPLC's false accusations is their hijacking of GuideStar USA. GuideStar is a database of more than two million nonprofit and non-governmental (NGO) organizations. It's considered the foremost authority on nonprofits, and had a self-avowed reputation for "remaining neutral."

A leftwing activist, Jacob Harold, came on board GuideStar in 2012. Mr. Harold, whose bio boasts of donating to the Obama campaign, extensive activism on behalf of climate change groups, and hosting a NARAL Pro-Choice D.C. men's event, tweeted a photo of himself holding a sign protesting President Trump at the radical Women's March in January 2017.[8] Except for Vermont ice cream magnates Ben and Jerry, it might be hard to find a more radical major CEO. So it's no wonder that Mr. Harold welcomed the SPLC as an authority. Using the SPLC's "hate map" as a resource, GuideStar smeared 46 organizations, many of them Christian, as "hate groups."

On June 21, 2017, a group of 41 Christian and conservative leaders, including former Attorney General Edwin Meese, signed a letter to GuideStar demanding deletion of the defaming labels, which GuideStar did—sort of.[9] The labels were removed but the damage was done and the information is available upon request.

Liberty Counsel, a Christian legal foundation, filed a defamation lawsuit on June 28, 2017 in the U.S. District Court for the Eastern District of Virginia against GuideStar for posting a label on Liberty Counsel's GuideStar page describing it as an SPLC-designated "hate group."

## D. James Kennedy Ministries Files Suit

On August 23, 2017, D. James Kennedy Ministries went straight to the original perpetrator, filing a federal lawsuit against the SPLC itself for defamation. In a letter to ministry supporters, president and CEO Dr. Frank Wright explained the reasons for taking this action:

> D. James Kennedy Ministries was classified as a hate group [by the SPLC] based on our position on LGBT (lesbian, gay, bisexual, transgender) issues. But our position here is inextricably intertwined and connected to our religious theology. It is not, never has been, and never will be based on hatred or violence. It is based wholly and completely on the never-failing Word of God (Leviticus 18:22, Romans 1:26-27, 1 Timothy 1:8-11, Mark 10:6-8, 1 Corinthians 6:9-11).
>
> The loss of funds from the program and the false and defamatory attacks are hurtful, but **the biggest issue here is the reckless attack against our Biblical beliefs and the concerted effort to disgrace, ridicule, and silence Christians for what they believe.** *The damage to our ministry's name and reputation is inestimable.*

As the suit filed against the Southern Poverty Law Center in the U.S. District Court in Alabama stated:

> Because the SPLC previously published material that evidenced hostility toward the Ministry, because of the extreme "Hate Group" language used by the SPLC, because of the extensive publication of the Hate Map through the use of the Internet and the SPLC Transmissions, and because the SPLC's conduct in making these publications was beyond reckless for the falsity of the information, the SPLC's conduct in publishing the Hate Map and SPLC Transmissions constitutes common-law malice.

## The SPLC's True Motives*

In 2014, the F.B.I. dropped the SPLC as a source for identifying hate groups. In March 2016, the U.S. Justice Department accused SPLC attorneys of "lack of professionalism" and "misconduct" for falsely characterizing the Federation for American Immigration Reform and the Immigration Reform Law Institute as "hate groups."

If there is still doubt as to the SPLC's motives, it was laid to rest in an interview with SPLC Senior Fellow Mark Potok, who said that his group's "hate group" criteria "have nothing to do with criminality or violence or any kind of guess we're making about 'this group could be dangerous.' It's strictly ideological."[10] Mr. Potok also stated, "Sometimes the press will describe us as monitoring hate crimes and so on. I want to say plainly that our aim in life is to destroy these groups, to completely destroy them."[11]

Ricardo Davis, an African-American who is the president of Georgia's Right-to-Life, also chairs the Constitution Party of Georgia, which is on the SPLC's hate list as "antigovernment." Interviewed by DJKM's Jerry Newcombe for a video program on the SPLC, Davis said that Dr. Martin Luther King's civil rights movement was undergirded by faith in God and in the Bible. In contrast, what the SPLC is promoting today often contradicts God's Word:

> If I could say something to [SPLC co-founder] Morris Dees right now, what I would say is, "Morris, you came alongside my father's generation to help them get out from under injustice, and it was unjust because it violated God's Word . . . but now, you're on the wrong side of history." [12]

---

* For more on the SPLC, please see the D. James Kennedy Ministry video "Profit$ of Hate," and the ministry's book, *The Southern Poverty Law Center Exposed.*

## CHAPTER 8

# RESPONDING WITH TRUTH AND GRACE

One reason Christians find themselves under unwarranted attack is as old as Creation: envy.

Cain slew Abel merely because he was insanely jealous that God was pleased by his brother Abel's sacrifice and not his (Genesis 4:8).

In the Book of Daniel, we read that Daniel was so successful in administering King Darius' kingdom that other court officials plotted to get rid of him, eventually coming up with a plan to frame him.

"Sometimes, people can hate us, not for doing anything wrong, but rather, for doing everything right," wrote Dr. Kennedy in one of his devotions.

> Shakespeare said, 'Envy doth merit, as its shade [shadow] pursue.' Envy pursues after merit, even as our shadow pursues us everywhere we go. And so, if you would be meritorious, if you would rise so much as an inch or two above the common herd, you will find that envy will be hard on your heels and breathing down your neck and blowing its hot flame breath singeing the hairs on the back of your neck.
>
> And so it was with Daniel; and so it has ever been. Daniel was preferred. Daniel had an excellent spirit. Daniel was envied; and Daniel was conspired against to pull him down.
>
> One theologian noted there is a certain tendency in evil that always wants to pull that which is good down to its own level. Evil is egalitarian. Evil men

want to make everyone else just as evil as they are.

But conforming to the world in order to dispel envy is not an option for a believing Christian. Instead, we must respond in ways that surprise our antagonists. For example, when an angry person says, "You church goers are all a bunch of hypocrites," you might try responding, "You're right! And there's always room for one more! Why don't you join us?"

This is similar to the spirit of the bumper sticker that says "Christians aren't perfect, just forgiven." It's a statement of humility and vulnerability, which are difficult to attack.

## Be a Conduit for Jesus' Love

The need for true humility—neither feigned nor exaggerated—cannot be overemphasized. Otherwise, we are rightly seen as holier-than-thou finger pointers. Non-believers are always on the lookout for spiritual arrogance in order to discredit Christianity. If we harbor such pride or contempt for others who don't share our faith, it is quite noticeable. The best way to overcome negative feelings toward others is to ask Jesus to allow us to be conduits of His love—right on the spot.

Since we're all guilty of sin, we need to keep the knowledge of grace close to our hearts. Only with God's help can we rise above what the world expects as a response to angry accusations. Proverbs 15:1 (ESV) advises that, "*A soft answer turns away wrath, but a harsh word stirs up anger.*" When someone insults us and we respond with a word of sympathy toward them instead of a pithy shot in return, it takes the wind right out of their sails. The best outcome is that they will want what we have, and this may well provide an opening to share the Gospel.

"This world does not operate on grace; it operates on the basis of merit, on the basis of justice," wrote Dr. Kennedy. "Quid pro quo, this for that; you do this, you get that. That is the way the entire world operates—on the basis of justice or equity. Early in my ministry, I went to preach in a jail, and a man snapped at me that all he demanded was justice. I said if he got justice, the floor would open up and send him to hell. What we need is mercy, not justice."

When we extend mercy to others, it is hard to ignore. Often, the most effective response to a false accusation is simply personal testimony. People can argue indefinitely about theological concepts, but a simple recitation of what Jesus has done for us is compelling and irrefutable.

When we reflect on how much God loves us, it is easier to love others, even the unlovable. One thing that indirectly refutes the charge that Christians are full of hate is acts of service. It stretches credibility to condemn as "haters" those who are serving meals to the poor, volunteering at hospitals, and showing everyday kindness.

*"Dear children, let us not love with words or speech, but with actions and in truth"* (1 John 3:18).

## Accusations and Responses

When false charges are leveled, here are some practical ways to respond. Keep in mind that truth in love is powerful in any situation.

*Accusation: You Christians hate homosexuals.*

**Answer:** Christians are admonished to love everyone as Christ loves us. That does not mean we must approve of every behavior, especially those that the Bible tells us are not only sinful but extremely harmful to individuals, families, and communities. Do you think it's "hateful" to oppose, for instance, prostitution, alcohol abuse or drug addiction? We think it is hateful to encourage such behavior.

*Accusation: Christians are lacking in compassion. By refusing to accept same-sex marriage you hurt people's feelings and makes them feel like second-class citizens.*

**Answer:** Which is more compassionate? Cheering people on to engage in harmful, sinful behavior, or trying to warn them about the consequences? God gave us rules for living because He loves us, not because He is a cosmic killjoy. Marriage since the beginning has always been the union of male and female: "*So God created man in his own image, in the image of God he created him; male and female he created them*" (Genesis 1:27 ESV), which Jesus Himself reaffirmed when He said, "*Have you not read that he who created them from the beginning made them male and female?*" (Matthew 19:4, ESV).

Also, it's not "hate" to maintain basic facts. For instance, putting up a barrier to jumpers on the Empire State Building is not "hatred" against those who don't believe in gravity. And maintaining that marriage, by definition, is the union of one man and one woman, as it has been throughout human history, is not "hate" against people who don't believe it or futilely try to redefine it. The only way human beings can reproduce is through the joining of male and female, which establishes the obvious design of marriage. Pretending otherwise does not make it so. Counterfeit money is not money, and counterfeit marriage is not marriage.

**Accusation: *Who are you to judge others? Jesus said, "Judge not, lest ye be judged."***

**Answer:** You're right. No one should judge others, since no one knows what is in someone else's heart. But we must judge behaviors as to whether they are healthy or helpful or not. We are all sinners. But the Bible is clear about right and wrong. God wants the best for us. It's not "hateful" to support values that benefit everyone.

This verse, one of the world's favorites, is also taken out of context. Jesus is warning against making hypocritical judgments—forbidding to others what we ourselves secretly engage in. "*For with the judgment you pronounce you will be judged*" (Matthew 7:2 ESV). Jesus says elsewhere, "*Do not judge by appearances, but judge with right judgment*" (John 7:24 ESV). Far from a call for absolute tolerance of all behaviors, Jesus' words actually implore us to make proper judgments sincerely and consistently about behaviors in accordance with God's Word.

**Accusation: Jesus said, "He who is without sin, cast the first stone."**

**Answer:** Yes, and it's a good thing He did, because we are all guilty of sin, and He loved us even while we rejected Him. He also told the woman caught in adultery, "*Go and sin no more*." She had hurt herself and others, and Jesus wanted her to start living a better, fuller life.

Christians don't wish to issue judicial punishments for sin; they wish in love to call sinners to repentance and salvation.

**Accusation: Christians hate transgendered people and will not accept them for who they are.**

**Answer:** God is clear that we should love people regardless of their state of mind, but it is not compassionate to aid and abet a delusion about someone's sexuality, especially for impressionable children who may never get the chance to mature enough to live according to their birth sex.

Dr. Paul R. McHugh, professor emeritus of psychiatry at Johns Hopkins University, has long campaigned against sexual reassignment surgery:

> Policy makers and the media are doing no favors either to the public or the transgendered by treating their confusions as a right in need of defending rather than as a mental disorder that deserves understanding, treatment, and prevention. This intensely felt sense of being transgendered constitutes a mental disorder in two respects. The first is that the idea of sex misalignment is simply mistaken—it does not correspond with physical reality. The second is that it

can lead to grim psychological outcomes.

Furthermore, "gender" is a false, 20<sup>th</sup> century construct. Our sex is a biological fact, given to us by God. "Male and female he made them." This fact is intuitively obvious to all of us, which is why we have to go through such contortions to deny it.

*Accusation: "You're on the wrong side of the homosexual/transgender issue now just like you were on the wrong side of civil rights in the 20<sup>th</sup> century because of your bigotry."*

**Answer:** Unfortunately, some Christians were indeed on the wrong side because they selectively used the Bible to support slavery and segregation. Christians are subject to sin like everyone else. But Bible-believing Christians were also the backbone of the civil rights movement. Martin Luther King, Jr. appealed mostly to the Bible in arguing for equality. By contrast, one would be hard-pressed to find approval of homosexual relationships and transgenderism in the Bible (indeed there are explicit warnings against them), whereas the texts on the equal dignity of all human beings created in the image of God are manifest and ultimately proved persuasive.

*Accusation: Christians don't care about the environment.*

**Answer:** Christians believe in the God-ordained human mission of being stewards of God's creation. This means that man, while dominant over all other living things (Genesis 1:26), is also charged with being a good steward of the home God has given us. Many Christians, such as Theodore Roosevelt, took conservation to be a God-given responsibility.

*Accusation: Christians who want to make abortion illegal hate and want to oppress women.*

**Answer:** It's the people who promote and profit from abortion that evidently hate women. Every abortion claims two victims: mother and child. The child loses his or her life, and the mother suffers emotional, psychological, and sometimes physical damage. Women who have undergone abortions need our compassion, and to know that God still loves them and will forgive them if they seek Him. Abortion is the world's cruel answer to difficult situations, but we believe its days are numbered. Science is proving beyond the shadow of a doubt that a unique human life exists from the moment of conception. Facilitating the brutal invasion of a woman's womb in order to kill her child is the opposite of compassion.

## A Final Word

It's not "hate" to disagree with someone. If it is, then we're all guilty at any given time, since people differ in their opinions. Biblically, love is seeking someone's ultimate good, and hate is seeking their harm.

Proverbs 13:24 (ESV) says, *"Whoever spares the rod hates his son, but he who loves him is diligent to discipline him."* To allow someone to persist in something that is destructive to him or her is *truly* hateful.

As stated in the introduction, the world seeks vengeance, returning hate for hate; the Christian is told to return love for hate and to work toward redemption of our enemies. We should never forget that at one time we lived in enmity against God. But even while we were His enemies, He sent His Son to die on the cross that we might be redeemed from our sinful state of hatred towards Him to live eternally in heaven with Him.

We know that the Father in Heaven sees all, and ultimately He will send His Son to earth again, and this time every knee shall bow before Him and every tongue confess that He is Lord to the glory of God the Father (Philippians 2:9-11). Let us, therefore, continue to counter lies and hate in the best possible way— with truth and grace.

# END NOTES

## Introduction

1   C.S. Lewis, from Book 3, Chapter 17, "Forgiveness," in *Mere Christianity* (1952), p. 59, PDF version, DACC.edu at: https://www.dacc.edu/assets/pdfs/PCM/merechristianitylewis.pdf.

2   From Spurgeon's Gems: 13, 14, cited in Quote Investigator, https://quoteinvestigator. com/2014/07/13/truth/ (accessed November 28, 2017).

## Chapter 1

1   Billy Graham, "Things God Hates," *Decision Magazine*, August 25, 2011, https:// billygraham.org/decision-magazine/september-2011/things-god-hates/ (accessed November 28, 2017).

## Chapter 2

1   Michael Weiskopf, "Energized by Pulpit or Passion, the Public Is Calling," *The Washington Post*, February 1, 1993, https://www.washingtonpost.com/archive/politics/1993/02/01/ energized-by-pulpit-or-passion-the-public-is-calling/f747ded3-b7c5-4578-ad3b-2f500dbaeacf/?utm_term=.e687421d9dc0 (accessed November 29, 2017).

2   Howard Kurtz, "Evangelical Outrage," *The Washington Post*, February 6, 1993, https://www. washingtonpost.com/archive/lifestyle/1993/02/06/evangelical-outrage/c6704db3-0f79-452d-bb5d-6da3bdc36202/?utm_term=.fab7a925d229.

3   Weiskopf, "Energized."

4   Kurtz, "Evangelical Outrage."

5   Ibid.

6   Elise Viebeck and Tom Hamburger, "Roy Moore: Alabama Voters Will 'See Through this Charade' of Sexual Misconduct Claim,'" *The Washington Post*, November 11, 2017, https:// www.washingtonpost.com/powerpost/roy-moore-alabama-voters-will-see-through-this-charade-of-sexual-misconduct-claims/2017/11/11/47218cde-c6e5-11e7-84bc-5e285c7f4512_ story.html?utm_term=.907478a10758 (accessed November 29, 2017).

## Chapter 3

1   William L. Shirer, *The Rise and Fall of the Third Reich: A History of Nazi Germany*, (New York: Simon and Schuster, 1960), 97.

2   "The Strange Life and Works of H.S. Chamberlain," in Shirer, 104-110.

3   Ibid, 107.

4   Ibid.

5   Ibid, 105.

6   Ibid.

7   Ibid, 108.

8   Mary Mills, "Propaganda and Children During the Hitler Years," The Nizkor Project, 1991-2012, http://www.nizkor.org/hweb/people/m/mills-mary/mills-00.html (accessed November 29, 2017).

9   Ibid.

10  Shannon Quinn, "The Eternal Jew," in "Top 10 Nazi Propaganda Films," January 1, 2017, Listverse, https://listverse.com/2017/01/01/top-10-nazi-propaganda-films/ (accessed November 29, 2017).

11  Ibid, "Heimkehr" at: https://listverse.com/2017/01/01/top-10-nazi-propaganda-films/.

12  Shirer, see "The Control of Press, Radio, Films," 244-248.

13  Shirer, 431.

14  "Kristallnacht," Holocaust Encyclopedia, United States Holocaust Museum, https://www.ushmm.org/wlc/en/article.php?ModuleId=10005201 (accessed November 29, 2017).

15  Terese Pencak Schwartz, "The Holocaust: Non-Jewish Victims," Jewish Virtual Library, http://www.jewishvirtuallibrary.org/non-jewish-victims-of-the-holocaust (accessed November 28, 2017).

16  Shirer, 240.

17  "Martin Niemöller: 'First, they came for the socialists...,'" United States Holocaust Museum, https://www.ushmm.org/wlc/en/article.php?ModuleId=10007392# (accessed November 28, 2017).

18  "The Truth about Jim Crow," The American Civil Rights Union, 2015, at: http://www.theacru.org/jimcrow/.

## Chapter 4

1   Massachusetts Governor's Hate Crimes Task Force report (2001).

2   "FBI Releases 2016 Crime Statistics," September 25, 2017, Federal Bureau of Investigation National Press Office, Washington, D.C., https://www.fbi.gov/news/pressrel/press-releases/fbi-releases-2016-crime-statistics (accessed November 28, 2017).

3   "2016 Hate Crime Statistics," Uniform Crime Reporting Program report for 2016, Federal Bureau of Investigation, Washington, D.C., https://ucr.fbi.gov/hate-crime/2016/topic-pages/incidentsandoffenses (accessed November 28, 2017).

4   Population Clock, United States Census Bureau, https://www.census.gov/popclock/ (accessed November 28, 2017).

5   Abigail Hauslohner, "Hate Crimes Reports Are Soaring, but We Still Don't Know How Many People Are Victimized," The Washington Post, November 17, 2017, https://www.washingtonpost.com/news/post-nation/wp/2017/11/17/hate-crimes-are-soaring-but-we-still-dont-know-how-many-people-are-victimized/?utm_term=.66eeeecae598 (accessed November 28, 2017).

## Chapter 5

1   Mary Eberstadt, "Regular Christians Are No Longer Welcome in American Culture," Time, June 29, 2016, http://time.com/4385755/faith-in-america/ (accessed November 28, 2017).

2   Frank Newport, "Most Americans Still Believe in God," Gallup News, June 29, 2016, http://

news.gallup.com/poll/193271/americans-believe-god.aspx (accessed November 28, 2017).

3   Eberstadt, "Regular Christians Are No Longer Welcome."

4   Joe Carter, "Debatable: Is the Christian Church a 'Hate Group'?" *The Gospel Coalition,* August 19, 2012, https://www.thegospelcoalition.org/article/debatable-is-the-christian-church-a-hate-group/ (accessed November 28, 2017).

5   Paul Bedard, "Support for Southern Poverty Law Center Links Scalise, Family Research Council Shooters," *The Washington Examiner,* June 14, 2017, http://www.washingtonexaminer.com/support-for-southern-poverty-law-center-links-scalise-family-research-council-shooters/article/2625982 (accessed November 28, 2017).

6   Ann E. Marimow, "Family Research Council shooter sentenced to 25 years," *The Washington Post,* September 19, 2013, https://www.washingtonpost.com/local/2013/09/19/d0df61f2-2131-11e3-b73c-aab60bf735d0_story.html?utm_term=.464f27dedb54 (accessed November 28, 2017).

7   Ann E. Marimow, "Family Research Council shooter pleads guilty to three felonies," *The Washington Post,* February 6, 2013, at: https://www.washingtonpost.com/local/family-research-council-shooter-pleads-guilty-two-three-felonies-including-terrorism-charge-in-federal-court/2013/02/06/aa2086b2-7075-11e2-ac36-3d8d9dcaa2e2_story.html?utm_term=.f0131fcb6cb9.

8   Paul Bedard, "Support for Southern Poverty Law Center."

9   Sara Sidner, Kyung Lah, Steve Almasy and Ralph Ellis, "Oregon Shooting: Gunman was Student in Class Where He Killed 9," CNN, October 2, 2015, http://www.cnn.com/2015/10/02/us/oregon-umpqua-community-college-shooting/index.html (accessed November 28, 2017).

10  Cheryl K. Chumley, "Devin Patrick Kelley: An Anti-Christian, Atheist 'Outcast'", *The Washington Times,* November 6, 2017, https://www.washingtontimes.com/news/2017/nov/6/devin-patrick-kelley-anti-christian-atheist-outcas/ (accessed November 28, 2017).

11  Ibid.

12  Josh Meyer, "FBI, Homeland Security Warn of More 'Antifa' Attacks," *Politico,* September 1, 2017, https://www.politico.com/story/2017/09/01/antifa-charlottesville-violence-fbi-242235 (accessed November 28, 2017).

13  Ibid.

14  Jessica Mendoza, "What is Antifa—and Does its Rise Mean the Left is Becoming More Violent?" *The Christian Science Monitor,* September 22, 2017, at: https://www.csmonitor.com/USA/2017/0922/What-is-antifa-and-does-its-rise-mean-the-left-is-becoming-more-violent; John Blake, "When Christians become a 'hated minority'," CNN Blog, May 5, 2013, http://religion.blogs.cnn.com/2013/05/05/when-christians-become-a-hated-minority/ (accessed November 28, 2017).

## Chapter 6

1   Jeff Carlson, "Gramsci, Alinsky and the Left," *themarketsworkblog,* February 11, 2017, https://www.themarketswork.com/2017/02/11/gramsci-alinsky-the-left/ (accessed November 28, 2017).

2   Paul Kengor, *Takedown: From Communists to Progressives, How the Left Has Sabotaged Family and Marriage,* (Washington, D.C.: WND Books, 2015), 92-104.

3   Ibid, 115-126.

4    "Summary of the U.S. Supreme Court Decision in *Christian Legal Society Chapter of the University of California, Hastings College of the Law v. Martinez,*" American Council on Education, http://www.acenet.edu/news-room/Documents/Summary-of-Decision-in-Christian-Legal-Society-Chapter-of-the-University-of-California,-Hastings-College-of-Law-v-Martinez.pdf (accessed November 28, 2017).

5    Peter Hassan, "California to Have Harsher Penalty for Pronoun Violations than for Knowingly Spreading HIV," *The Daily Caller,* October 9, 2017, http://dailycaller.com/2017/10/09/california-to-have-harsher-penalty-for-pronoun-violations-than-for-knowingly-spreading-hiv/ (accessed November 28, 2017).

6    Ibid.

7    George Orwell, *1984* (New York: Signet Classic edition, New American Library, 1961), 232.

## Special Insert 2

1    Saul Alinsky, *Rules for Radicals: A Pragmatic Primer for Realistic Radicals,* (New York: Vintage Books, 1971).

2    Hillary Rodham, "There Is Only the Fight," a thesis for the Bachelor of Arts Degree in the Special Honors Program, Wellesley College, May 2, 1969, at: https://nukegingrich.files.wordpress.com/2007/08/hillaryclintonthesis.pdf (accessed November 28, 2017).

3    Matt Patterson, "Study Saul Alinsky to Understand Barack Obama," *The Washington Examiner,* February 6, 2012, http://www.washingtonexaminer.com/study-saul-alinsky-to-understand-barack-obama/article/243226 (accessed November 28, 2017).

4    *Rules for Radicals,* 130.

5    James Lewis, "Barack Obama and Alinsky's Rules for Psychopaths," *American Thinker,* September 25, 2008, http://www.americanthinker.com/articles/2008/09/barack_obama_and_alinskys_rule.html (accessed November 28, 2017).

6    *Rules for Radicals,* 128.

7    Ibid, 152.

8    Ibid, 73.

9    Ibid, 136.

## Chapter 7

1    Jessica Chasmar, "Ben Carson Placed on Southern Poverty Law Center's 'Extremist' Watch List," *The Washington Times,* February 8, 2015, https://www.washingtontimes.com/news/2015/feb/8/ben-carson-placed-on-southern-poverty-law-centers-/ (accessed November 28, 2017).

2    Ibid.

3    Joe Schoffstall, "Southern Poverty Law Center Transfers Millions in Cash to Offshore Entities," *Washington Free Beacon,* August 31, 2017, http://freebeacon.com/issues/southern-poverty-law-center-transfers-millions-in-cash-to-offshore-entities/ (accessed November 28, 2017).

4   Carl M. Cannon, "The Hate Group that Incited the Middlebury Melee," *RealClearPolitics. com*, March 19, 2017, https://www.realclearpolitics.com/articles/2017/03/19/the_hate_group_that_incited_the_middlebury_melee_133377.html (accessed November 28, 2017).

5   "Hate Map," Southern Poverty Law Center, https://www.splcenter.org/hate-map (accessed November 28, 2017).

6   Carl M. Cannon, "The Hate Group that Incited the Middlebury Melee."

7   Tyler O'Neil, "Scalise Shooter 'Liked' the Terror-Linked SPLC, Which Repeatedly Attacked Scalise," *PJ Media*, June 22, 2017, https://pjmedia.com/trending/2017/06/22/scalise-shooter-liked-the-terror-linked-splc-which-repeatedly-attacked-scalise/ (accessed November 28, 2017).

8   Bob Unruh, "GuideStar Sued for Using Far-Left 'Hate' Labels," *WorldNetDaily.com*, June 28, 2017, http://www.wnd.com/2017/06/guidestar-sued-for-using-far-left-hate-labels/ (accessed November 28, 2017).

9   Susan Hogan, "After Conservative Backlash, Charity Tracker GuideStar Removes 'Hate Group' Labels," *The Washington Post*, June 26, 2017, https://www.washingtonpost.com/news/morning-mix/wp/2017/06/26/after-conservative-backlash-charity-tracker-guidestar-removes-hate-group-labels/?utm_term=.383269dc08fa (accessed November 28, 2017).

10  Tyler O'Neil, "Southern Poverty Law Center: 'Our Aim in Life Is to Destroy These Groups, Completely,'" *PJ Media*, September 1, 2017, https://pjmedia.com/trending/2017/09/01/southern-poverty-law-center-our-aim-in-life-is-to-destroy-these-groups-completely/ (accessed November 28, 2017).

11  Ibid.

12  Jerry Newcombe, "What Is Hate And Who Defines It? The SPLC?", *DJamesKennedy.org*, August 23, 2017, https://www.djameskennedy.org/article-detail/what-is-hate-and-who-gets-to-define-it-the-splc (accessed November 28, 2017).

## Chapter 8

1   D. James Kennedy, "Being Envied for Righteous Living," Devotions, https://www.djameskennedy.org/devotional-detail/20171109-being-envied-for-righteous-living (accessed November 28, 2017).

2   D. James Kennedy, "Don't Confuse Justice with Mercy," Devotions, https://www.djameskennedy.org/devotional-content (accessed November 28, 2017).

3   Dr. Paul McHugh, "Transgender Surgery Isn't the Solution," *The Wall Street Journal*, May 13, 2016, https://www.wsj.com/articles/paul-mchugh-transgender-surgery-isnt-the-solution-1402615120 (accessed November 28, 2017).